U.S. Government Q&A!

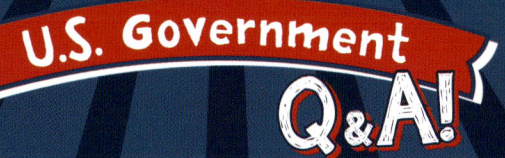

What Are STATES' Rights?

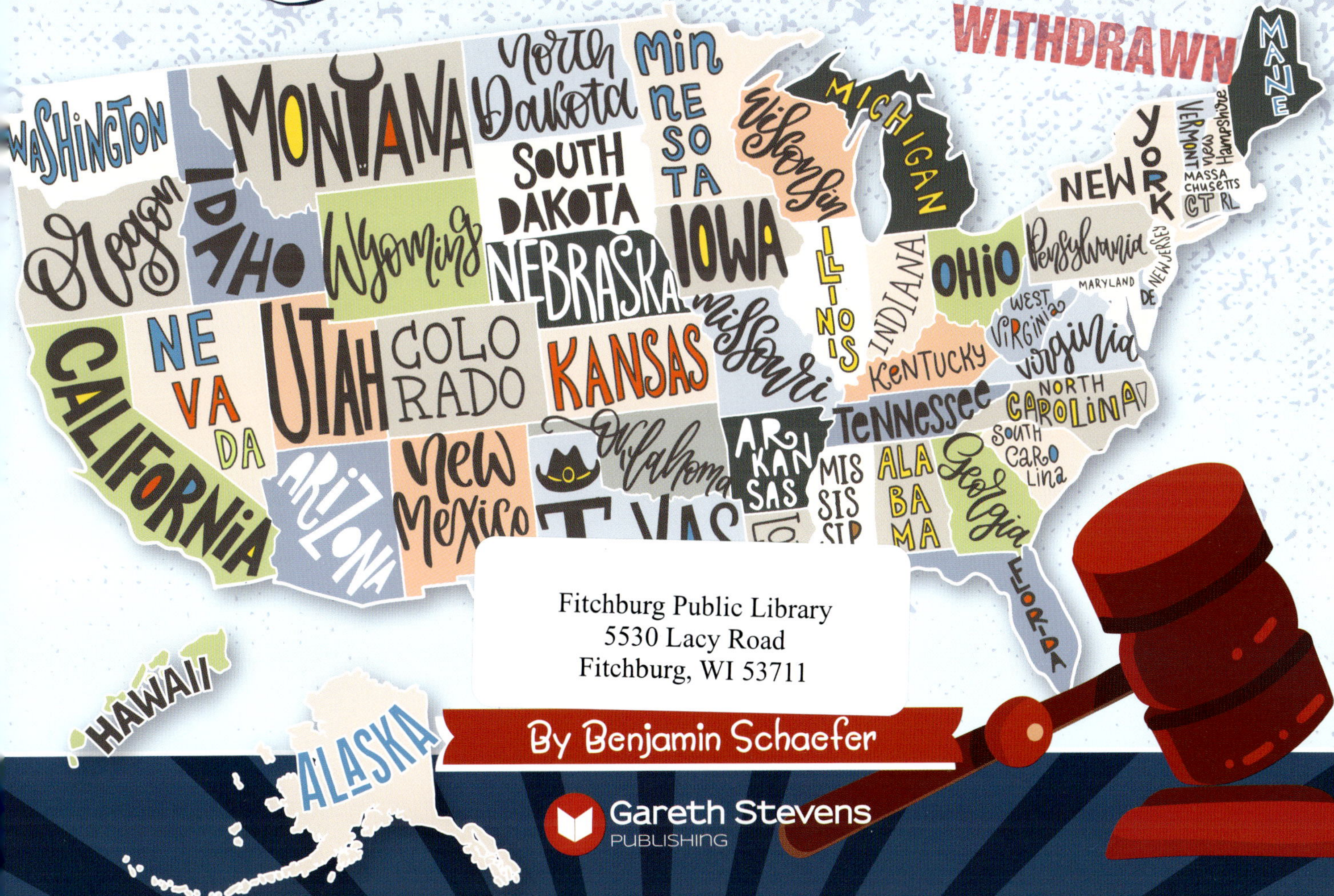

By Benjamin Schaefer

Gareth Stevens PUBLISHING

Please visit our website, www.garethstevens.com. For a free color catalog of all our high-quality books, call toll free 1-800-542-2595 or fax 1-877-542-2596.

Library of Congress Cataloging-in-Publication Data

Names: Schaefer, Benjamin Mark, author.
Title: What are states' rights? / Benjamin Schaefer.
Description: New York : Gareth Stevens Publishing, 2022. | Series: U.S. government Q & A | Includes index.
Identifiers: LCCN 2020033677 (print) | LCCN 2020033678 (ebook) | ISBN 9781538264270 (library binding) | ISBN 9781538264256 (paperback) | ISBN 9781538264263 (set) | ISBN 9781538264287 (ebook)
Subjects: LCSH: States' rights (American politics)–Juvenile literature. | Federal government–United States–Juvenile literature.
Classification: LCC JK311 .S27 2022 (print) | LCC JK311 (ebook) | DDC 320.473/049–dc23
LC record available at https://lccn.loc.gov/2020033677
LC ebook record available at https://lccn.loc.gov/2020033678

First Edition

Published in 2022 by
Gareth Stevens Publishing
29 E. 21st Street
New York, NY 10010

Copyright © 2022 Gareth Stevens Publishing

Designer: Andrea Davison-Bartolotta
Editor: Charlie Light

Photo credits: Cover (map), p. 1 (map) KateChe/Shutterstock.com; cover (gavel), p. 1 (gavel) Svetlana Shamshurina/Shutterstock.com; series art (paper, feather) Incomible/Shutterstock.com; series art (blue banner, red banner, stars) pingbat/Shutterstock.com; p. 5 joecicak/E+/Getty Images; p. 7 GraphicaArtis/Getty Images; pp. 9, 13 Everett Collection/Shutterstock.com; p. 11 (main) ungvar/Shutterstock.com; p. 11 (inset) MPI/Getty Images p. 15 (main) Hulton Archive/Getty Images; pp. 15 (pins), 19 (pins) Alexander Limbach/Shutterstock.com; p. 16 pyzata/Shutterstock.com; p. 17 Rusty Russell/Getty Images; p. 19 (main) Keystone/Getty Images; p. 21 Nik Merkulov/Shutterstock.com.

All rights reserved. No part of this book may be reproduced in any form without permission in writing from the publisher, except by a reviewer.

Printed in the United States of America

Some of the images in this book illustrate individuals who are models. The depictions do not imply actual situations or events.

CPSIA compliance information: Batch #CSGS22: For further information contact Gareth Stevens, New York, New York at 1-800-542-2595.

Find us on

Contents

The First Try 4
Let's Try This Again 6
Flexibility Is Key 8
The Reserved Powers 10
Speak Out! 12
The Civil War and States' Rights 14
Taking on Taxes 16
The State of Education 18
The Environment 20
Glossary 22
For More Information 23
Index 24

Words in the glossary appear in **bold** type the first time they are used in the text.

The First Try

During the American Revolution, the war in which the colonies became independent, the colonists created a "firm **league** of friendship" called the United States of America.

The Articles of Confederation created this league and was the first U.S. constitution, or piece of writing that states the nation's laws. It gave most governing powers to the states and didn't allow the federal, or national, government to tax people. At that time, the nation owed a lot of money and was close to falling apart!

Government Guides

Article III of the Articles of Confederation stated that the "league of friendship" would provide colonists "common defense [guard from enemies], the security of their liberties, and their mutual [shared] and general welfare."

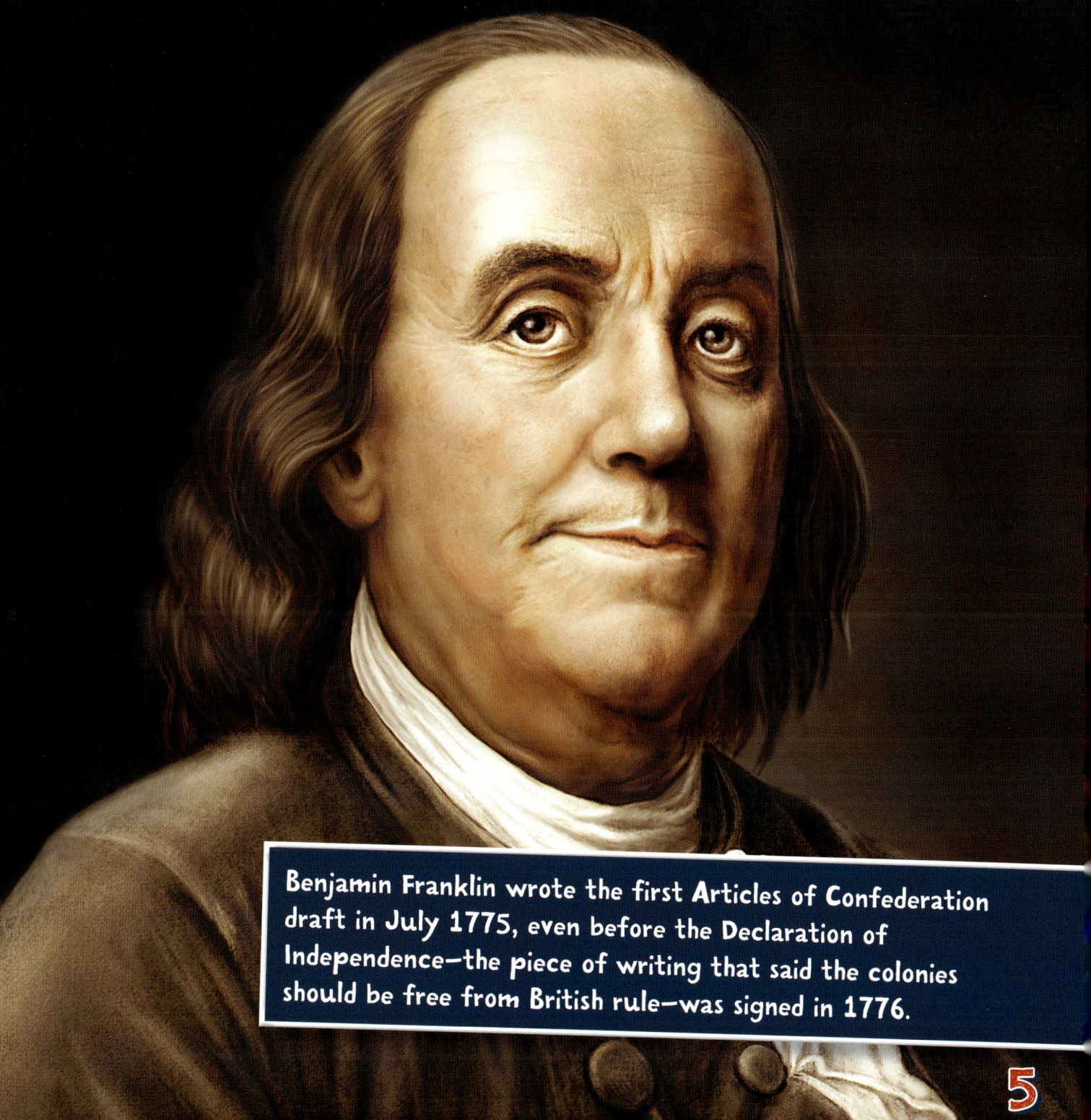

Benjamin Franklin wrote the first Articles of Confederation draft in July 1775, even before the Declaration of Independence—the piece of writing that said the colonies should be free from British rule—was signed in 1776.

Let's Try This Again

To fix the Articles of Confederation, 55 men met in 1787 for the **Constitutional Convention**. The men, who became known as founders, knew that they needed to find a **compromise** that would give both the federal government and state governments enough power—but not too much. This was a new idea called Federalism. The founders wrote the idea into a new U.S. Constitution.

Federalism allows states to pass their own laws and have their own powers. The United States federal government has the right to get involved when needed.

Government Guides

James Madison said that state government powers "are numerous and **indefinite**."

Alexander Hamilton recognized the limits of the Articles of Confederation and was one of several Founding Fathers key to creating today's U.S. Constitution during the Constitutional Convention.

Flexibility Is Key

The new Constitution gave the federal government certain powers, including printing money, declaring—or announcing—war, and creating the post office. When necessary, the **Elastic Clause** allowed the federal government to create new powers including a national bank and taxes. Some feared the national government had too much power, though.

The Bill of Rights is the first 10 amendments, or additions, to this Constitution. The Tenth Amendment says that any powers not given to the government by the Constitution are "reserved," or saved, for the states.

Government Guides

"The powers not delegated [assigned] to the United States by the Constitution, not prohibited [not allowed] by it to the States, are reserved to the states, respectively, or to the people."
—Tenth Amendment, the last amendment in the Bill of Rights.

A Bill of Rights had to be added to the U.S. Constitution before all the states ratified, or approved, it. James Madison wrote the Bill of Rights and presented it on June 8, 1789.

The Reserved Powers

The Constitution doesn't say what these "reserved" powers are, but many of them have become state laws over the years. Precedent, or tradition, has made them a part of state governments across the country.

Some of these reserved powers are infrastructure (intrastate highways and roads), commerce within the state (the way that you buy things), traffic laws, and elections. We're going to look at times when state powers **conflicted** with federal powers, and how these reserved powers affect your everyday life.

Government Guides

"No position appears to me more true than this; that the general [national] government cannot effectually [effectively] exist without reserving to the states the possession [ownership] of their local rights."
–Charles Pinckney, signer of the Constitution

The founders made the Constitution a little unclear on purpose, allowing for it to grow and change, and for states to have power when they needed it.

signing of the Constitution

Speak Out!

The first time that the states and the federal government fought over their rights was in 1798, when the Alien and Sedition Acts were passed. These laws made it harder for **immigrants** to vote and for people to speak out against the federal government.

Founding Fathers Thomas Jefferson and James Madison wrote **resolutions** in Kentucky and Virginia that supported the rights of states to nullify, or say no to, federal laws they didn't see as fair. These resolutions led to a justification, or cause, for the Civil War.

Government Guides

"I see, as you do, and with the deepest affliction [sadness], the rapid strides [speed] with which the federal branch of our government is advancing towards the usurpation [taking] of all the rights reserved to the states."
–Thomas Jefferson

Thomas Jefferson spoke out against the federal government taking power from the states. He also spoke out against slavery, even though he owned over 600 **enslaved** African people himself. States' rights to practice slavery sparked the Civil War.

The Civil War and States' Rights

When the country was founded, slavery was allowed in every state. As the country grew, Northern states started to make it illegal. Southern states fought for slavery to continue.

People argued over whether new states should be slave-holding or "free." In 1860, Abraham Lincoln, who believed the federal government should prevent new states from being slave-holding, won the presidency. Southern states began to **secede** from the Union in order to keep the state power to own enslaved people. This led to the Civil War.

Government Guides

Carl Schurz said that enslavers made slavery an issue of states' rights, then "raised the threat [danger] of separation, secession, [and] disunion, in order to enforce its [their] demands."

Carl Schurz believed in state rights and was also an abolitionist, meaning he wanted slavery ended. He considered it important for states to speak out against the national laws allowing slavery.

Taking on Taxes

One of the most important reserved powers is taxation. Although the federal government also has taxation power, states have always had the right to collect a variety of taxes. One of the most common taxes is the "sales tax." Sales tax is a percentage, or part, of the cost of something you buy that then goes to the state government to pay for these services.

Taxes are used to pay for public services, including schools and health benefits. They also pay for police.

public school building

States have the right to tax their citizens, and citizens have the right to protest, or strongly oppose, taxes. Here, citizens protest a suggested income tax in Tennessee.

The State of Education

Another reserved state power is control over education. It affects how many tests you take, how much money your school gets, when your school year starts, and importantly, your rights at school.

The federal and state governments had a conflict over this power in a Supreme Court case called *Brown v. Board of Education*. The Supreme Court is the highest federal court. It decided that **segregation** based on race in public schools is not legal, and that **integration** is the way forward.

Supreme Court Justice Earl Warren wrote that in public schools, "'separate but equal' has no place" and segregated schools "are inherently [naturally] unequal."

Thurgood Marshall was the lawyer, or person who helps others with problems with the law, who won the important *Brown v. Board of Education* case. It showed the limits of state rights in cases of education.

The Environment

The Supreme Court has also found that states have the power to control activities that can harm the environment, or the natural world. This means states can pass their own laws in order to keep their air and water clean.

Sometimes, this means that what's legal in one state isn't legal in another. Take fracking, for example. This practice includes shooting water at rock to break it up, then collecting the natural gas below. Maryland, New York, Massachusetts, and Vermont have passed laws banning fracking for safety reasons.

Think About It!

What are some recent examples of state power being in conflict with federal government power? Have there been any recent problems where states have had to take control?

State Reserved and Shared Powers

States have the power to create and control:

- schools
- local governments
- business within the state
- marriage laws
- public safety
- elections

States share power with the federal government to:

- collect taxes
- borrow money
- create banks
- create courts
- oversee public health and safety
- enforce laws

The balance between federal and state powers in the United States continues to change. Powers they share are called concurrent powers.

Glossary

compromise: a way of two sides reaching agreement in which each gives up something to end an argument

conflict: to be in an opposing way that prevents agreement. Also, a strong argument.

Constitutional Convention: a meeting that took place in 1787 to address problems in the original U.S. constitution

elastic: able to return to an original shape after being stretched

enslaved: the state of being "owned" by another person and forced to work without pay

immigrant: one who comes to a country to settle there

indefinite: an uncertain amount

integration: the act of opening a group, community, or place to all people

league: a united group of nations or people

resolution: an official statement of purpose voted on by a group

secede: to leave a country

segregation: the forced separation of races or classes

For More Information

Books

Barcella, Laura. *Know Your Rights!: A Modern Kid's Guide to the American Constitution.* New York, NY: Sterling Children's Books, 2018.

Hooks, Gwendolyn. *If You Were a Kid During the Civil Rights Movement.* New York, NY: Children's Press, 2017.

Lyman, Geraldine P. *Powers of the People: A Look at the Ninth and Tenth Amendments.* New York, NY: PowerKids Press, 2019.

Websites

BrainPop Social Studies – the U.S. Constitution
brainpop.com/socialstudies/ushistory/usconstitution/
Learn more about the United States Constitution with videos and quizzes!

Ducksters: U.S. Government Tenth Amendment
ducksters.com/history/us_government/tenth_amendment.php
Join the Ducksters team in learning more about how the Tenth Amendment helps define federal and state powers.

Young Voices For the Planet
youngvoicesfortheplanet.com/for-kids/
This site teaches kids how to get involved in the environmental movement.

Publisher's note to educators and parents: Our editors have carefully reviewed these websites to ensure that they are suitable for students. Many websites change frequently, however, and we cannot guarantee that a site's future contents will continue to meet our high standards of quality and educational value. Be advised that students should be closely supervised whenever they access the internet.

Index

abolitionist 15
Alien and Sedition Acts 12
American Revolution 4
Articles of Confederation 4, 5, 6, 7
Bill of Rights 8, 9
Brown v. Board of Education 18, 19
citizens 17
Civil War 12, 13, 14
colonists 4
commerce 10
concurrent powers 21
Constitution 6, 7, 8, 9, 11
Declaration of Independence 5
elections 10, 21
Federalism 4
fracking 20
Franklin, Benjamin 5
Hamilton, Alexander 7
infrastructure 10

Jefferson, Thomas 12, 13
Lincoln, Abraham 14
Madison, James 6, 9, 12
Marshall, Thurgood 19
money 4, 8, 18, 21
Pinckney, Charles 10
police 16
post office 8
protest 17
reserved powers 10, 16
sales tax 16
school 16, 18, 21
Schurz, Carl 14, 15
slavery 13, 14, 15
Supreme Court 18, 20
taxes 8, 16, 17, 21
Tenth Amendment 8, 9
traffic laws 10
Warren, Earl 18